EARLY
SHELBY COUNTY
ALABAMA

MARRIAGES
- 1825-1869 -

**Compiled By:
Nell Motes Goggans**

SOUTHERN HISTORICAL PRESS
INC.
Book Publishers

**Southern Historical Press, Inc.
Greenville, South Carolina**

Please direct all correspondence and book orders to:
SOUTHERN HISTORICAL PRESS, Inc.
1071 Park West Blvd.
Greenville, SC 29611

Originally Published 1961
ISBN #978-1-63914-193-7
Printed in the United States of America

PREFACE

Shelby County was formed in 1818 from part of Montgomery County, that was formed in 1816 from part of Monroe County. Monroe County was formed in 1815 from part of Washington County, Mississippi Territory and the Creek Cession of 1814. Columbiana is the county seat of Shelby County.

This book contains marriage records as recorded in the first book of marriages in Shelby County, plus some of the early marriages recorded in later volumes. They were copied from a photostatic typewritten copy of the original records in the possession of the Department of Archives and History in Montgomery, Alabama.

The original records are old and the handwritten, spidery script, was hard to interpret. It is possible the copist was not able to decipher all of the spelling correctly.

The records from December 1827 to September 1837 are not recorded, Very few marriages prior to 1827 are recorded. It appears this book of marriages was compiled at a later date from the original records. Perhaps, by then some of the original records were lost.

The bridegrooms are listed alphabetically in this book. The bride's index begins on page 80.

Nell Motes Goggans
(Mrs. L. L. Goggans)

November 1961
Epes, Alabama

ADAMS, J. C. and C. E. SENTELL
7 December 1858. Volume II, page 352.

ADAMS, Joseph Mann and Martha F. BONCHER
22 September 1852. Volume II, page 114.

ADAMS, L. E. and J. D. BYERS
24 March 1868. Volume IV, page 203.

ADAMS, SILAS and Jane STRAIN
19 November 1850. Volume II, page 6.

ADAMS, Tilman and Elizabeth E. STRADNER
13 July 1862. Volume III, page 164.

ADAMS, William C. and Mary E. WOODS
20 October 1864. Volume III, page 216.

ADAMS, W. W. and S. E. WOOD
9 November 1866. Volume III, page 340.

ADAWAY, HARDY and Francis MOORE
11 October 1868. Volume IV, page 77.

ADCOCK, Johnathan and Rhoda E. JONES
15 February 1865. Volume III, page 229.

ADKINS, A. M. and Susan VINES
30 May 1868. Volume IV, page 58.

ADKINS, James and Sarah HARRIS
15 September 1859. Volume III, page 60.

ADKINSON, William J. and Sarah L. MARDIS
20 December 1856. Volume II, page 269.

AGEE, Noah A. and Ann C. HUNLEY
29 November 1854. Volume II, page 190.

ALEXANDER, George H. and Nancy A. JONES
11 March 1860. Volume III, page 89.

ALEXANDER, Robert T. and Martha THOMAS
8 March 1863. Volume III, page 179.

ALLEN, James and Eveline NABORS
26 November 1843. Volume I, page 147.

ALLEN, James R. and Mary Jane BRASHER
13 March 1859. Volume II, page 360.

ALLEN, Jeremiah and Mariah LOLLY
26 June 1842. Volume I, page 113.

ALLEN, Jesse and Elizabeth MORRIS
9 July 1849. Volume I, page 238.

ALLEN, John and Virginia C. JOHNSON
23 January 1842. Volume I, page 101.

ALLEN, John and M. J. SMITH
4 February 1866. Volume III, page 362.

ALLEN, John and R. THAMES
25 October 1866. Volume III, page 338.

ALLEN, John A. and Harriett MULLINS
18 November 1855. Volume II, page 220.

ALLEN, John A. and Susan L. MULLINS
2 August 1854. Volume II, page 155.

ALLEN, John R. and Remelia GOTHARD
16 August 1868. Volume IV, page 70.

ALLEN, Preston and Rhody C. BYRUM
20 November 1856. Volume II, page 259.

ALLEN, Robert and Nancy HUNICUTT
24 December 1845. Volume I, page 147.

ALLEN, Spencer and LeLiah FULLER
17 May 1845. Volume I, page 202.

ALLEN, Spencer B. and Mary Jane JOHNSON
23 November 1843. Volume II, page 179.

ALLEN, William M. and Charlotte N. Leeper
7 March 1859. Volume II, page 366.

ALLEN, William and Mary SAWYER
17 December 1867. Volume IV, page 55.

ALLEN, William M. and Pricillia L. JOHNSON
2 November 1854. Volume II, page 179.

ALLEN, Wilson and Letty WILLIAMS
1 May 1856. Volume II, page 238.

ALLEN, Young and Phereba BISHOP
18 June 1843. Volume I, page 137.

ALPHIN, Julius and Martha PHILIN:
29 December 1840. Volume I, page 52.

ALTON, James M. and Rhody A. PAIGN
27 November 1851. Volume II, page 41.

AMBERTSON, Asa and Maggie B. GALBERTH
1 August 1866. Volume III, page 332.

ANDERSON, James D. and Racheal L. KING
24 September 1864, Volume III, page 112.

ANDERSON, Richard and Jane GRIMES
22 August 1857. Volume IV, page 182.

ANDERSON, T. A. and Amanda SIMONS
13 July 1854. Volume II, page 156.

ANDREWS, James E. and Susan V. CROSS
6 February 1866. Volume II, page 234.

ANDREWS, Sebert and C. L. FAULKNER
19 June 1858. Volume II, page 345.

ANDREWS, W. L. and Narcissa C. DeSHAZO
15 July 1858. Volume II, page 329.

ANDREWS, William F. and Eliza J. HUBBARD
11 January 1856. Volume II, page 227.

ANDREWS, Williamson and Rutha A.E.R. HOLLI
16 May 1855. Volume II, page 195.

ANGLINE, Thomas N. and Lucinda LEEPER
4 June 1857. Volume II, page 286.

ARGO, Nimrod and Elizabeth FOSTER
10 June 1855. Volume II, page 196.

ARLIDGE, M. C. and A. S. ROBERSON
20 July 1865. Volume III, page 224.

ARMSTRONG, Asa and Jane QUINN
4 March 1841. Volume I, page 56.

ARMSTRONG, Elias and Louisa GRIMES
20 August 1854. Volume II, page 107.

ARMSTRONG, Elias and Mary E. GOLD
4 March 1849. Volume I, page 212.

ARMSTRONG, Hiram and L. A. EAST
30 August 1866. Volume III, page 374.

ARMSTRONG, John and Sarah S. SIMMONS
25 January 1844. Volume I, page 155.

ARMSTRONG, John and Nancy WEBB
4 November 1855. Volume II, page 219.

ARMSTRONG, John W. and Rebecca FREEMAN
25 February 1864. Volume III, page 195.

ARMSTRONG, LEVI R. and Elizabeth PARKER
22 June 1854. Volume II, page 151.

ARMSTRONG, Martin and Mary E. Grimes
24 July 1850. Volume I, page 361.

ARMSTRONG, Rufus and Eliza A. SEALE
29 October 1850. Volume II, page 7.

ARMSTRONG, Wesley and Sarah A. PRICE
14 January 1866. Volume III, page 305.

ARMSTRONG, Williamd and Louisa SEALE
16 February 1851. Volume II, page 15.

ARMSTRONG, Woodson and Ellen E. VANSANT
23 May 1854. Volume II, page 149.

ARMSTRONG, William A. J. and Sarah C. BUSBY
11 October 1867. Volume IV, page 168.

ARNETT, James C. and Lolly HORTON
9 September 1851. Volume II, page 30.

ARNETT, Westley W. and Mary SPARKS
5 January 1862. Volume III, page 148.

ARNOLD, Jesse and Mary ROGERS
6 January 1826. Volume I, page 17.

ARNOLD, William J. and Sarah A. McGRADY
1 January 1860. Volume IV, page 28.

ASH, William and Permelia GILBERT
8 January 1841. Volume I, page 60.

ASH, William G. and Susan C. GILBERT
19 March 1846. Volume I, page 69.

ASHCRAFT, James W. and Martha EDMONDSON
16 September 1852. Volume II, page 71.

ASKINS, Dennis and Manda WELLS
24 December 1840. Volume I, page 49.

ATCHISON, James and Amdand DeSHAZO
11 September 1850. Volume I, page 259.

ATCHISON, Jackson, and Christiana WEAVER
25 September 1861. Volume III, page 138

ATKINSON, BENJAMIN F. and Nancy MULLINS
21 March 1850. Volume I, page 257.

ATKINSON, William W. and Barbary DRAKE
17 August 1845. Volume I, page 208.

ATKINSON, Robert and Martha KURNER
12 September 1861. Volume III, page 136

ATTAWAY, John and Mary COX
2 November 1867. Volume IV, page 162.

ALBRIGHT, Rufus and Mary Ann FREEZE
8 December 1853. Volume II, page 133.

AUTURY, Bushrod and Dicy CRUMPTON
5 April 1867. Volume IV, page 191.

AVERETT, G. and Mary P. JORDAN
13 February 1849. Volume I, page 214.

AVERY, Duke and Bethana S. THOMAS
8 October 1851. Volume II, page 37.

AVERY, E. D. and Nancy L. COKER
23 December 1855. Volume II, page 221.

AVERY, George and Mary REDDING
28 December 1846. Volume I, page 329.

AVERY, Levy and Frances PHIGREEN
3 June 1866. Volume III, page 322.

AVERY, Robert and Sally A. THOMAS
16 November 1851. Volume II, page 38.

AVERY, W. N. and Tebitha THOMAS
24 December 1846. Volume I, page 283.

BAGGETT, John D. and Dorothy VICK
11 October 1860. Volume III, page 104.

BAGGETT, T. C. and Isabella VICK
23 February 1864. Volume III, page 199.

BAILEY, Bryant and Tilda SACKES
29 May 1869. Volume IV, page 126.

BAILEY, Ervin and Caroline E. JONES
13 December 1853. Volume II, page 134,

BAILEY H. H. and M. S. BAILEY
5 April 1848. Volume II, page 337.

BAILEY, Henderson and Aurena LEE
30 August 1841. Volume I, page 78.

BAILEY, John S. and Nancy PATTON
17 November 1859. Volume III, page 73.

BAILEY, Joseph C. and Celest JONES
7 December 1865. Volume III, page 279.

BAILEY, Mardis and Amanda PAYNE
14 November 1844. Volume I, page 183.

BAILEY, Needham and Winifred LEE
9 April 1857. Volume II, page 288.

BAILEY, Robert and Mary FORD
26 April 1848. Volume I, page 19.

BAILEY, Seveir and Nancy ALEXANDER
    7 January 1844. Volume I, page 165.

BAILEY, Thomas and Mary A. Acton
    28 December 1843. Volume I, page 166.

BAILEY, THomas N. and S. C. BAILEY
    3 December 1865. Volume III, page 291.

BAILEY, William H. and Susan Jane ACTON
    15 February 1844, Volume I, page 161.

BAILEY, William J. and Sarah E. BAILEY
    23 July 1867. Volume IV, page 180.

BAILEY, William L. and Margaret JONES
    18 December 1856. Volume II, page 267.

BAILY, Ausburn and Annie LEE
    25 December 1849. Volume I, page 232.

BAILY, Bennett, H. and Racheal JONES
    14 November 1861. Volume III, page 142

BAILY, James L. and Nancy LOVELESS
    6 November 1854. Volume II, page 167.

BAILY, John A. and Mary M. PERRY
    24 July 1856. Volume II, page 250.

BAILY, P. J. and Harriett BAILY
    9 September 1858. Volume II, Page 337.

BAILY, Thomas and Louisa JONES
    18 September 1860. Volume III, page 10

BAILY, Thomas F. and Carolina JONES
    17 January 1853. Volume II, page 139.

BAKER, Charles W. and Frances C. VANDIVER
    22 June 1862. Volume III, page 163.

BAKER, George M. and Elizabeth SMITH
30 July 1859. Volume III, page 54.

BAKER, James and Elizabeth C. BAXLEY
3 November 1859, Volume III, page 71.

BAKER, James and Elizabeth TEAGUE
27 January 1842. Volume I, page 92.

BAKER, James H. and Mary A. BUSBY
20 February 1866. Volume III, page 312.

BAKER, John H. and Mary C. VANDIVER
3 November 1864. Volume III, page 2.

BAKER, Leonard J. and Racheal TEAQUE
13 October 1853. Volume II, page 117.

BAKER, Samuel and Elizabeth C. NABORS
29 January 1857. Volume II, page 274.

BALDWIN, Mannon and Elizabeth CRANFORD
16 March 1865. Volume III, page 231.

BALDWIN, Taylor and Mary BARGERS
25 November 1868. Volume IV, page 80.

BALLARD, A. W. and Rebecca A. ROBERTSON
12 November 1863. Volume III, page 185.

BANDY, James A. and M. C. NABORS
25 September 1859. Volume III, page 64.

BANISTER, Ike and Susan CLAYTON
10 October 1868. Volume IV, page 84.

BARBER, Green B. and Sarah Ann GOODGAME
30 October 1845. Volume I, page 234.

BAREFIELD, John and Sarah A. SMITH
21 May 1854. Volume II, page 148.

BARKER, Sterling and Nancy ELLIOTT
   23 April 1846. Volume I, page 257.

BARNETT, Charles and Eleanor B. OWENS
   28 April 1858. Volume II, page 321.

BARNETT, Charlie and Susan HUGHS
   24 June 1864. Volume III, page 276.

BARNETT, George D. and Sarah F. Johnson
   19 March1868. Volume IV, page 204.

BARNETT, Joel and Elizabeth HUGHES
   29 January 1865. Volume III, page 227.

BARNETT, John and Mary E. RAY
   19 July 1868. Volume IV, page 66.

BARNS, Gabrel and Eliza JORDAN
   14 September 1845. Volume I, page 252.

BARRETT, Benjamin and Martha BELLINS
   13 February 1865. Volume III, page 235

BARRETT, James and Martha E. ELLISON
   29 September 1861. Volume III, page 13

BARRETT, John and Martha GOWINS
   30 December 1847. Volume I, page 290.

BASS, Samuel and A. M. LEE
   1 August 1866. Volume III, page 333.

BASSETT, Henry and Lelah SCOGGINS
   16 January 1865. Volume III, page 225.

BATES, James and Amanda McKEE
   3 December 1855. Volume II, page 212.

BATES, James and Matilda J. TALBOT
   25 July 1860. Volume III, page 116.

BATES, James R. and Anna C. TEMPLE
7 December 1854. Volume II, page 169.

BATES, Martin and Sarah E. MAHAN
14 April 1859. Volume III, page 53.

BATES, Thomas J. and Caroline HAND
9 January 1853. Volume II, page 104.

BATES, Thomas J. and Hetty BEARDEN
4 June 1865. Volume III, 239.

BATSON, David and Nancy PUTMAN
31 October 1867. Volume IV, page 168.

BATSON William and Sarah E. PACE
4 December 1859. Volume III, page 75.

BATTON, Thomas T. and Rhody BREWER
29 November 1859. Volume III, page 75.

BATY, Green and Ninna ROBBINS
2 November 1848, Volume I, page 207.

BAUGH, Joseph and M. DYKES
1 November 1866. Volume III, page 338.

BAXLEY, William D. and Letty COMER
15 March 1859. Volume II, page 369.

BAXTLEY, Henry and Martha WEBSTER.
26 October 1858. Volume II, page 343.

BAZZELL, John G. and Catherine COGGINS
16 September 1855. Volume II, page 210.

BEAM, Hiram and Lucy GREEN
2 July 1865. Volume III, page 242.

BEAN, James and Rebecca WILLINGHAM
18 April 1869. Volume IV, page 122.

BEAN, W. H. and Mary T. ROBINSON
3 March 1867. Volume III, page 369.

BEARDEN, Reeves M. and Eliza HORTON
8 June 1856. Volume II, page 243,

BEARDIN, Valentine and Hetty MORRIS
14 November 1850. Volume II, page 8.

BEARDING, Arthur and Rebecca WHITFIELD
10 December 1840. Volume I, page 58.

BEASLEY, David C. and Betheny J. AVERY
19 August 1858. Volume II, page 329.

BEASLEY, John and Penelope E. PHILGREEN
30 October 1855. Volume II, page 226.

BEASLEY, Parker and Mary Ann CUNNINGHAM
29 April 1841. Volume I, page 66.

BEASLEY, William and Lydia E. AVERY
28 October 1851. Volume II, page 38.

BEASLY, Henry N. and Mary A. WEBB.
19 September 1855. Volume II, page 210.

BEAVERS, Thomas H. and Amanda L, DICKINSON
23 August 1855. Volume II, page 203.

BEAY, Thomas and Martha J. MONEY
14 February 1866. Volume III, page 307

BELL, James M. and Jane MULLINAX
27 September 1840. Volume II, page 46

BELL, William H. and Anna FORSHEE
22 May 1842. Volume I, page 105.

BENNER, Charles L. and Elizabeth GRIMES
22 December 1858. Volume II, page 347.

BENNETT, Madixa and Jane GAMBLE
   22 July 1841. Volume I, page 71.

BENSON, Enoch and Mary McCLELLEN
   26 January 1863. Volume III, page 180.

BENSON, Henry and Eleanor LITTLEFIELD
   12 November1854. Volume II, page 186.

BENTLEY, Joseph G. and Maud H. MORGAN
   6 March 1853. Volume II, page 88.

BENTLY, Eli. and Sarah E. HORTON
   16 June 1858. Volume II, page 323.

BENTON, Columbus and Margaret OLDHAM
   2 October 1865. Volume II, page 264.

BENTON, Franklin and Julia Ann JOHNS
   7 September 1854. Volume II, page 160.

BENTON, James and Frances FAUST
   21 October 1858. Volume II, page 338.

BENTON, James and Carolina NASH
   25 June 1845. Volume II, page 240.

BERRY, J. W. and Maria F. MONEY
   23 December 1856. Volume II, page 261.

BEVELL, James and Martha ALLEN
   20 April 1843. Volume I, page 134.

BEVELL, Wyatt and Mary Ann SHRADNER
   7 March 1843. Volume I, page 129.

BEVILL, William F. and Sarah A. GLOVER
   10 June 1850. Volume I, page 146.

BEVILL, William M. and Delila A. HARPER
   23 December 1846. Volume I, page 239.

BEVILL, B. and Ruthia COST
22 March 1849. Volume I, page 212.

BEVILL, Barden and Ann MILLS
14 March 1847. Volume I, page 250.

BEVILL, John G. and Mary Ann HARPER
25 July 1848. volume I, page 198.

BEVILL, R. D. and Mary GREGORY
9 January 1848. Volume I, page 293.

BILLERY, George and Sarah E. DAVIS
10 November 1850. Volume II, page 17.

BILLINGSLEA, Robert J. and Emely C. CROSS
5 November 1843. Volume I, page 145.

BINSON, Thomas J. and C. COLLINS
5 November 1868. Volume IV, page 85.

BIRCHFIELD, Benjamin and Elizabeth HIDENS
6 June 1865. VolumeIII, page 239.

BIRCHFIELD, Elijah and Dorothy BLACKSBY
25 February1847. Volume I, page 194.

BIRD, Hilliard and M. A. McCLINTON
11 March 1855. Volume II, page 187.

BIRDEN, Richard and Margaret M. WHITFIELD
19 February 1852. Volume II, page 65.

BIRD, John and Sarah Ann GUYTON
4 November 1851. Volume II, page 34.

BISHOP, Henry and Margaret M. WILSON
28 October 1847. Volume II, page 187.

BISHOP, James and Adaline VINSON
8 September 1853. Volume II, page 110.

BISHOP, John and Sarah M. FULLHAM
7 December 1866. Volume III, page 341.

BISHOP, William M. and Martha PAYNE
1 July 1869. Volume IV, page 132.

BLACK, Jackson and Louisa HALL
29 August 1846. Volume I, page 265.

BLACK, James L. and Jane RICHEY
30 July 1856. Volume II, page 254.

BLACK, John and Clarisa DAVIDSON
2 September 1863. Volume III, page 172.

BLACK, Thomas and Susan WEAR
1 November 1867. Volume IV, page 166.

BLACKSBY, C. C. and Emily CARDIN.
5 October 1865. Volume III, page 256.

BLACKSBY, Henry and Delilah FARR
13 March 1845. Volume I, page 201.

BLACKBERRY, Jesse M. and Mary GARDNER
14 February 1850. Volume I, page 253.

BLACKERBY, Ben. F. and Mary J. THOMAS
7 March 1861. Volume III, page 124.

BLACKERBY, James P. and Mary SMITH
5 September 1844. Volume I, page 178.

BLAIR, William and Elizabeth J. TINNERY
16 January 1858. Volume II, page 305.

BLAKE, John R. and Elizabeth HENDERSON
24 December 1856. Volume II, page 261.

BLAKE, Thomas A. and Mary C. CALDWELL
23 June 1858., Volume II, page 325.

BLANKSHIP, Andrew and Sylvania DENNIS
20 February 1855. Volume II, page 190.

BLANKSHIP, John and Mary A. E. TYLER
9 May 1855. Volume II, page 193.

BLANKSHIP, John and Jane HARMEL
9 October 1852. Volume II, page 51.

BLANKSHIP, Reuben and Julia GRIFFIN
15 August 1865. Volume III, page 250.

BOMAN, Sanford and Leah WATERMAN
15 February 1849. Volume I, page 318.

BONN, John and Nancy C. GARNER
14 November 1867. Volume IV, page 157.

BOOTH, Izah and Jane LAWLEY
21 August 1851. Volume II, page 30.

BOOTH, John and Loujena CHAMPION
21 August 1851. Volume II, page 31.

BOOTH, William and Lucinda LAWLEY
21 August 1851. Volume II, page 30.

BOOTHE, James and Missouri LOLLEY
10 September 1854. Volume II, page 159

BOOTHE, James and Frances HYDE
29 September 1861. Volume III, page 13

BORMAN, John H. and Sarah A. FLORNEY
16 January 1845. Volume I, page 193.

BOTTOM, Thomas and Rhody S. BREWER
27 November 1859. Volume III, page 75.

BOWDON, Elbert and Margaret A. FROST
12 January 1854. Volume II, page 138.

BOWDON, Samuel F. and Margaret CUNNINGHAM
8 July 1857. Volume II, page 290.

BOWDON, William G. and Mary Jane SCOTT
5 December 1840. Volume I, page 130.

BOWERS, Albert and Caroline SUMMER
10 June 1867. Volume IV, page 157.

BOWMAN, J. Harvey and Caroline C. JONES
28 July 1864. Volume III, page 208.

BOYD, B. and Nancy H. LEE
2 June,1862. Volume III, page 162.

BOYD, Noah and Hannah JEMISON
31 October 1867. Volume IV, page 171.

BRADFORD, Harrison and Nancy J. SPARKS
12 October 1865. Volume III, page 370.

BRADFORD, John and Elvira HANDLEY
21 February 1845. Volume I, page 198.

BRADFORD, John and Nancy LOWERY
12 September 1825. Volume I, page 23.

BRADFORD, John H. and L. A. PARSON
21 June 1866. Volume III, page 222.

BRADFORD, Lenuel and Landonia NELSON
28 October 1859. Volume III, page 69.

BRADLY, John and Mary C. ROPER
4 June 1850. Volume I, page 222.

BRADLY, M. H. and Nancy Ann MARONEY
12 January 1855. Volume II, page 172.

BRADSHAW, William and E. FUNDERBURK
13 August 1865. Volume III, page 248.

BRAGG, Charles and Mary OLDHAM
7 February 1844.   Volume I, page 161.

BRANCH, Peter and Caldona HORTON
17 December 1846.   Volume I, page 146.

BRANTLEY, H. Joseph and Racheal LAMB
8 January 1864.   Volume III, page 194.

BRASHER, Alexander and Caroline BRASHER
11 February 1858.   Volume II, page 313.

BRASHER, Andrew J. and Sarah WIDDORE
8 May 1863.   Volume III, page 179.

BRASHER, Henry and Frances STUCNOR
19 June 1864.   Volume II, page 205.

BRASHER, Henry and Vina WARE
28 December 1865.   Volume IV, page 36.

BRASHER, Isham and Susannah M. STOKES
1 January 1856.   Volume II, page 224.

BRASHER, John and Frances D. KINDRICK
14 January 1855.   Volume II, page 180.

BRASHER, Joseph and Elenor JOHNSON
30 September 1847.   Volume I, page 186.

BRASHER, L. P. and Mary A, GOOCH
14 May 1844.   Volume I, page 169.

BRASHER, Leroy and Sarah Jane BROTHERS
7 June 1863.   Volume II, page 262.

BRASHER, Lewis T. and Elizabeth HOWARD
6 November 1856.   Volume III, page 178.

BRASHER, M. J. and Nancy DANIELS
3 February 1867,   Volume III, page 365.

BRASHER, Perry and Nancy J. WHITFIELD
28 August 1859. Volume III, page 56.

BRASHER, Richard and Clarinda PITTS
30 October 1860. Volume III, page 107.

BRASHER, Samuel and Margaret GOOCH
2 November 1840. Volume I, page 147.

BRASHER, Samuel and Cordelia POINDEXTER
17 April 1864. Volume III, page 201.

BRASHER, Seborn and Jane E. BRAGG
6 September 1860. Volume III, page 109.

BRASHER, Tom and Elizabeth DRAKE
30 July 1859. Volume III, page 55.

BRASHER, William J. and Mrs. Nancy GRIFFIN
16 May 1867. Volume IV, page 185.

BRASHER, Z. S. and Margaret E. HUGHES
9 January 1851. Volume II, page 10.

BRASHIRE, John M. and Mary WELDON
16 October 1851. Volume II, page 33.

BRASHWOOD, A. H. and Missouri JONES
3 November 1864. Volume III, page 218.

BRASURE, John J. and Elizabeth DOLLAR
4 May 1827. Volume I, page 14.

BREWER, Alexander and Nancy GOTHARD
9 May 1858. Volume II, page 319.

BRIDGES, James W. and Barnacy BENTON
3 May 1843. Volume I, page 135.

BRIDGES, John and Mary Frances RINEHART
26 April 1865. Volume III, page 237.

BRIDGES, John, Jun. and Sarah O'NEAL
1 November 1867. Volume IV, page 161.

BRIDGES, W. J. and Everline SEALE
7 June 1867. Voluem IV, page 64.

BRINKER, Albert J. and Louisa C. BEVILL
28 Novenber 1858. Volume II, page 346.

BRINKER, Joseph M. and Caroline ELLIOTT
11 September 1844. Volume I, page 187.

BRISON, Washington and Mary ACKER
30 January 1845. Volume I, page 229.

BRITTON, B. F. and Amanda LEE
21 July 1858. Volume II, page 330.

BRIZLEY, H. H. and Susan J. MARTIN
12 September 1861. Volume III, page 13

BROADHEAD, C. N. and Louisa LANHAM
1 April 1866. Volume III, page 318.

BROADHEAD, S. and L. Melissa LEMMONS
30 November 1855. Volume II, page 215.

BROCK, John H. and Sarah E. WOOD
10 January 1856. Volume II, page 242.

BROTHERS, Andrew J. and Sarah MULDORE
18 May 1863. Volume III, page 179.

BROWN, William E. and Mary FULTON
1 January 1842. Volume I, page 117.

BROWN, William E. and Mary WOODRUFF
22 July 1851. Volume II, page 26.

BRYAN, Aldon and Zilpha LEE
1 July 1852. Volume II, page 65.

BRYSON, William and Terissa ACKER
12 November 1840. Volume I, page 51.

BUCHANAN, Charles and Nancy HANSON
7 December 1846. Volume I, page 264.

BUCHER, Joseph and Martha F. MORGAN
5 June 1845. Volume I, page 203.

BULLOCK, Leonard and Margaret WELDON
15 May 1865. Volume III, page 234.

BURCHETT, Christopher and Caroline
HONEYCUTT. Volume I, page 121.

BURCHFIELD, Isaac and Esther BAKER
12 December 1844. Volume I, page 195.

BURCHFIELD, Isaac B. and Eleanor O'HARA
26 May 1857. Volume II, page 290.

BURFORD, John W. and Aveline COTHRAN
2 July 1844. Volume I, page 173.

BURGES, Joshua and D. A. ROACH
20 November 1851. Volume II, page 48.

BURK, James and Kezia WILSON
21 February 1850. Volume II, page 3.

BURK, James S. and Mary KING
10 May 1854. Volume II, page 175.

BURNETT, Absolum and Eliza LITTLEFIELD
21 August 1844. Volume I, page 182.

BURNETT, Bentley and Vina GRIFFIN
18 August 1867. Volume IV, page 175.

BURNETT, James and Martha COLLINS
16 July 1842. Volume I, page 128.

BURNETT, Lewis and Sarah BENSON
25 October 1865. Volume III, page 295.

BURNETT, Louis and Jane GENTRY
7 March 1867. Volume IV, page 202.

BURNETT, Lewis and Malinda TURNER
8 February 1864. Volume III, page 195.

BURNETT, Warren and Ellen ASKIN
16 April 1854. Volume II, page 146.

BURNS, Jackson and Elizabeth STAGMAN
18 September 1853. Volume II, page 113

BURNS, W. A. and A. A. VANDIVER
7 August 1866. Volume III, page 332.

BURR, Martin and Hannah MORGAN
24 August 1867. Volume IV, page 178.

BUZBEE, James and Manada PHELAN
19 August 19, 1841. Volume I, page 73.

BUZBEE, John H. and Martha HOWARD
17 March 1869. Volume IV, page 101.

BUZBY, John M. and Amanda R. THOMAS
21 January 1860. Volume II, page 320.

BUZBY, Mason H. and Mary E. COLLINS
1 July 1869. Volume IV, page 132.

BUZBY, William J. L. and Nancy COLMAN
15 January 1863. Volume III, page 178.

BUTLER, David C. and Margaret McCLANAHAN
4 November 1841. Volume I, page 44.

BUTLER, Richman and Mary C. LEONARD
23 May 1844. Volume I, page 177.

BUTLER, Thomas and Kiziah F. BEASLEY
    10 August 1865. Volume III, page 253.

BUTLER, Zachariah and Jane ROWLES
    8 March 1840. Volume I, page 35.

BUTT, Frederick and Louisa E. CANDIN
    12 March 1846. Volume I, page 281.

BUTTOM, Thomas C. and Kiziah BUZBY
    10 August 1865. Volume III, page 253.

BUZBY, Demsey and Fanny E. MARTIN
    14 August 1851. Volume II, page 42.

BUZBY, John A. and Rebecca JONES
    15 October 1840. Volume I, page 47.

BUZBY, Samuel and Amanda ARMSTRONG
    5 Ictober 1854. Volume II, page 165.

BYERS, Robert and Ann E. DRAKE
    19 May 1861. Volume III, page 130.

BYRUM, Isaac M. and Brenda HOLLINGSWORTH
    13 July 1865. Volume III, pagᵤ 244.

BYRUM, William A. and Martha J. GREEN
    13 July 1865. Volume III, page 243.

CALAWAY, Job and Matilda PAGE
    20 December 1850. Volume II, page 62.

CALDWELL, Alfred M. and Susan RUSHING
    16 July 1844. Volume I, page 171.

CALDWELL, David W. and Elizabeth BRASHER
    5 April 1855. Volume II, page 189.

CALDWELL, H. L. and Mattie LEE
    10 February 1865. Volume III, page 282.

CALDWELL, John and Harriett E. BAILEY
    2 February1851. Volume II, page 14.

CALDWELL, William and Elizabeth BAILEY
    10 January 1859. Volume II, page 372.

CAMERON, James A. and Susan L. LEE
    28 October 1867. Volume IV, page 171.

CAMPBELL, Asa and Mary RIDER
    11 September 1845. Volume I, page 256,

CAMPBELL, Jasper and Elizabeth BROADHEAD
    8 January 1859. Volume III, page 364.

CAMPBELL, Zeblin and Manoh READER
    11 October 1860. Volume III, page 105.

CAMRON, Benjamin B. and Elizabeth FREEZE
    11 June 1826. Volume I, page 16.

CANNIS, Thomas S. and Martha SWINEY
    27 June 1852. Volume II, page 61.

CANNON, William J. and Mollie E. PHILLIPS
    20 March 1867   volume IV, page 198.

CARDEN, L. L. and Mariah PITTS
    22 December 1864. Volume III, page 222

CARDEN, William M. and Jane H. USSERY
    16 September 1858. volume II, page 334

CARDIN, Charles M. and Barbara Ann STAGMAN
    3 January 1866. Volume III, page 350.

CARDIN, Phillip and Winifred WILLIS
    27 September 1865. Volume III, page 26

CARDIN, Phillip L. and Nancy A. GUY
    27 July 1854. Volume II, page 153.

CARDWELL, Bart and Mary B. CARD
12 May 1858. Volume II, page 308.

CARDWELL, Simeon and Mary F. HELTON
26 December 1860. Volume III, page 114.

CAREY, G. B. and Mary Jane BARFIELD
21 February 1859. Volume II, page 356.

CARLETON, John and Elizabeth Drake
17 June 1860. Volume II, page 202.

CARNES, Christopher and Elizabeth GARDNER
10 May 1852. VolumeII, page 57.

CAROTHERS, David H. and Mary J. HESTER
30 June 1842. Volume I, page 108.

CARR, Dennis and S. ANDERSON
23 December 1866. Volume IV, page 148.

CARR, James and Rebecca VICK
19 May 1842. Volume I, page 106.

CARR, William C. and Mary A. O'BARR
26 December 1867. Volume Iv, page 160.

CARTER, James and Laurana GLASCOCK
8 May 1864. Volume III, page 203.

CARTER, James H. and Mary E. GARDNER
4 February 1862. Volume III, page 121.

CARTER, William and Sarah J. HATCHER
29 January 1867. Volume Iv, page 53.

CARTER, Thomas and Mary Ann CARY
20 April 1865. Volume III, page 237.

CARVER, Isaac and Elizabeth CUMMINGS
10 May 1852, Volume II, page 58.

CASTON, E. W. and Sarah A. RACHEALS
1 May 1861. Volume III, page 129.

CAVANISS, Johathan and Elizabeth GREEN
31 August 1851. Volume II, page 37.

CHAMBERS, John and Lucretia McGUNNISS
2 January 1840. Volume I, page 22.

CHAMBERS, John F. and Camilla COLLINS
18 June 1857. Volume II, page 285.

CHAMBERS, John F. and Fannie V. CURTIS
22 June 1859. Volume II, page 370.

CHAMPION, F. M. and Elizabeth LUCUS
11 August 1866. Volume III, page 361.

CHAMPION, Jackson and Rebecca LAWLEY
15 September 1850. C Volume II, page 2

CHAMPION, Newton and Elizabeth LINDSEY
1 September 1851. Volume II, page 52.

CHEATHAM, John C. and Hester M. DAVIDSON
3 August 1860. Volume III, page 99.

CHESESS, A. and Mary MOLTON
14 December 1865. Volume III, page 298

CHESTER, William D. and Nancy G. BENSON
26 August 1847. Volume I, page 285.

CHILDERS, Joel and H. A. ROBERSON
1 November 1866. Volume III, page 334.

CLARK, Archer and Elizabeth CROWSON
13 March 1846. Volume I, page 270.

CLARY, George and Emmeline NASH
19 January 1867. Volume III, page 357.

CLARY, George and Mary HEFLIN
17 February 1863. Volume III, page 192.

CLEMENTS John and Lydia G. SETTERS
21 September 1863. Volume III, page 260.

CLEMENTS, Thomas and Emeline OVERTON
27 October 1843. Volume I, page 154.

CLUB, Daniel and Livly WAGGING
14 February 1854. Volume II, page 141.

COBB, John and Elizabeth McCASKILL
15 November 1849. Volume I, page 327.

COBB, William and Sarah McCASKILL
5 May 1850. Volume I, page 328.

COHILL, John M and Mary E. KIDD
25 September 1839. volume I, page 36.

COKER, D. P. and Telitha G. COBB
31 January 1850. Volume I, page 345.

COKER, Henry and Leucinda COBB
15 April 1853. Volume II, page 94.

COKER, James and Letitia HOLCOMB
25 December 1855. Volume II, page 217.

COKER, James, Jun. and Lettish WALLS
19 February 1858. Volume II, page 303.

COKER, James M. and Syntha THOMPKINS
7 April 1844. Volume I, page 170.

COKER, John W. and Sarah WALLS
6 August 1857. Volume II, page 294.

COKER, Joseph B. and Mary HOLCOMB
10 October 1861. Volume III, page 141.

COKER, Thomas A. and Irena AKINS
   2 November 1843. Volume I, page 148.

COLE, Thomas D. and Lolly Irene BUTLER
   23 June 1864. Volume III, page 204.

COLUM, William and Lucinda GLASSCOCK
   28 January 1847. Volume I, page 280.

COMER, C. C. and Elizabeth GARDNER
   10 May 1852. Volume II, page 52.

COMER, C.C. and Martha DUREN
   30 June 1859. Volume III, 57.

COMER, John T. and Martha LITTLEFIELD
   4 November 1858. Volume II, page 341.

CONDON, Calvin M. and Louisa E. SINGLETON
   22 June 1841. Volume I, page 84.

CONWALL, J. C. and Martha Shaw
   11 April 1867. Volume Iv, page 191.

COOK, John nad Samantha HENLEY
   30 July 1843. Volume I, page 143.

COOK, Walter and Cornelia C. MICKLE
   13 November 1853. Volume II, page 118.

COOPER, Bennett and Martha ELLISON
   14 December 1845. Volume I, page 235.

COOPER, James W. and Rebecca MULLINS
   23 September 1860. Volume III, page 10

COLLINS, Joel and Hannah BOSTON
   1 March 1830. Volume II, page 35.

COLLINS, John and Sarah A. BURNETT
   14 February 1858. Volume II, page 312.

COLLINS, Thomas and Sarah Ann RASBERRY
7 August 1848. Volume I, page301.

COLLINS, Thomas and Susan M. BEAN
16 December 1860. Volume III, page 118.

COLLINS, Thomas and Deliah ROBINSON
20 March 1848. Volume I, page 341.

COLLINS, William H. and Nancy FAULKNER
25 April 1858. Volume II, page 227.

COLLUM, Clark and Margaret STORY
23 July 1865. Volume III, page 246.

COLLUM, E. and Martha A. RAY
2 December 1855. Volume II, page 226.

COLLUM, George and Sarah GLASSCOCK
21 July 1864, Volume III, page 209.

COLLUM, Westley and Elizabeth COOK
12 October 1842. Volume I, page 115.

CORNELSON, John and Lucinda GILLEY
19 November 1840. Volume I, page 48.

COSHATT, John A. and Elizabeth HINTON
25 March 1855. Volume II, page 191.

COSHUTT, J. Shelby and Polly Ann KING
26 September 1858. Volume II, page 334.

COST, Elijah and Caroline RAY
26 September 1844. Volume I, page 186.

COST, James and Susan E. CROSS
17 August 1848. VolumeIpage 300.

COST, John and Martha JOHNSON
4 September 1845. Volume I, page 217.

COST, Thomas B. and F. M. McCLENDON
    11 August 1868. Volume IV, page 71.

COTTINGHAM, Washington and Lucinda WALDROP
    11 July 1841. Volume I, page 70.

COUCH, Samuel Hardy and Victoria MITTCHEL
    24 July 1858. Volume II, page 328.

COX, Lewis and Armentus SIMMONS
    23 December 1847. Volume I, page 291.

CRAIN, Harrison and Eliza Ann HALE
    6 July 1857. Volume II, page 302.

CRAIN, James and Elizabeth GRIFFIN
    22 June 1856. Volume II, page 247.

CRAWFORD, Robert and Eleanor NETTLES
    11 July 1846. Volume I, page 254.

CRAWFORD, Travis and Martha PREWETT
    15 February 1857. Volume II, page 277.

CRAWFORD, SOLOmon and Martha SPARKMAN
    5 August 1856. Volume II, page 254.

CRAWFORD, Washington and Mary MARTIN
    15 February 1857. Volume II, page 277.

CRIM, Abraham and Joana ARMSTRONG
    16 January 1830. Volume I, page 241.

CRIM, George and Susan WATSON
    21 April 1844. Volume I, page 172.

CRIM, JOhn H. and Emily CROWSON
    1 November 1840. Volume I, page 72.

CRIM, John W. and Harriett DANIELS
    15 July 1852. Volume II, page 67.

CRIM, John W. and M. C. RODGERS
16 June 1856. Volume II, page 370.

CRIM, Levi and Mary EVANS
23 June 1858. Volume II, page 327.

CRIM, Peter and Mary MARTIN
29 June 1867. Volume IV, page 183.

CRIM, Robert H. and Elizabeth MASON
16 July 1842. Volume I, page 243.

CRIM, Thomas C. and Anna WATSON
3 August 1851. Volume II, page 25.

CRIM, William and Caroline McDANIEL
23 March 1841. Volume I, page 62.

CRIM, Zachariah and Lucinda HUNNEYCUTT
21 December 1852. Volume II, page 82.

CRIMM, J. W. and Sarah A. MOORE
26 April 1846. Volume I, page 245.

CROCKETT, William and Mary Jane RICKEY
3 November 1841. Volume I, page 82.

CROMWELL, John T. and Catherine McCLANAHAN
26 April 1840. C Volume I, page 40.

CROMWELL, John T. and Dempsy STINSON
25 May 1864. Volume III, page 202

CROSS, Ben and Henrietta L. BOWDON
14 December 1854. Volume II, page 170.

CROSS, Richman C. and Martha LINDSEY
26 September 1844. Volume I, page 189.

CROSS, Rufus and Margaret SMITH
20 June 1861. Volume III, page 154.

CROSS, S. M. and Mary J. SENTELL
21 September 1865. Volume III, page 28

CROSS, William and Eliza BENSON
7 October 1841. Volume I, page 77.

CROSS, William L. and Sarah F. McADAMS
21 September 1858. Volume IIm page 335

CROSS, Zachariah and Malinda BENSON
18 September 1821. Volume I, page 74.

CROWSON, William B. and Armeta CROSS
30 September 1845. Volume I, page 217.

CRUMP, James P. and Louisa HARPER
21 December 1837. Volume I, page 150.

CRUMPTON, Edmond and Matilda WILLIAMS
10 July 1849. Volume I, page 327.

CUMINS, Thomas and Mary SWINNEY
10 May 1852. Volume II, page 271.

CURTIS, John and Sarah A. CARDIN
9 July 1858. Volume II, page 328.

CURTIS, Joseph E. and Louisa MARDIS
2 February 1856. Volume II, page 222.

CUSHATT, J. A. and Caroline LUCUS
3 December 1846. Volume I, page 259.

DALRYMPLE, Thomas H. and Sara Ann MARTIN
28 September 1851. Volume II, page 41.

DAVENPORT, Henry M. and Eliza CRIM
1 September 1861. Volume III, page 135

DAVIS, Bennett M. and Sophia ELLIOTT
11 October 1849. Volume I, page 356.

DAVIS, Christopher and Sarah A. BAKER
18 November 1841. Volume I, page 87.

DAVIS, Edward and Mary C. PERRY
31 October 1859. Volume II, page 70.

DAVIS, Henry and Carolina MARTIN
11 January 1849. Volume I, page 317.

DAVIS, James B. and Mahala GREEN
6 August 1844. Volume I, page 170.

DAVIS, James H. and Frances MIDDLEBROOKS
13 December 1840. Volume I, page 64.

DAVIS, John and Nancy RAY
21 December 1844. Volume I, page 188.

DAVIS, Nevil and Mary A. MARTIN
17 August 1862. Volume III, page 176.

DAVIS, URiah and Tabitha MORRIS
13 July 1845. Volume I, page 210.

DAVIS, William H. and Luvina LAWLEY
18 November 1841. Volume I, page 93.

DAVIS, William and Rebecca MASON
21 July 1853. Volume II, page 106.

DAVIS, William C. and Nancy M. VICE
21 July 1852, Volume II, page 63.

DENIS, William C. and Margaret LEMELEY
25 November 1839. Volume I, page 22,

DENNIS, Jackson and Nancy VINES
12 August 1852. Volume II, page 62.

DeSHAZO, Elbert H. and Elizabeth Gambol
15 June 1845. Volume I, page 207.

DeSHAZO, James L. and Monah OVERTON
     23 December 1861. Volume III, page 158

DeSHAZO, John M. and Elizabeth LEE
     26 September 1858. Volume II, page 335

DeSHAZO, William C. and Amanda C. DELOACH
     24 April 1856. Volume II, page 244.

DeSHAZO, William K. and Mary A. HOWARD
     15 July 1858. Volume II, page 329.

DILL, Stepehn F. and Elizabeth GRIFFIN
     22 May 1863. Volume III, page 178.

DOAKE, L. D. and Lucinda ARNETT
     29 January 1842. Volume I, page 99.

DOLLAR, Ambros and Lucinda GLOVER
     17 February 1842. Volume I, page 101.

DOLLAR, John and Catherine WILLIAMSON
     14 May 1846. Volume I, page 275.

DONELY, Noah and Sarah JOHNSTON
     13 February 1845. Volume I, page 196.

DOSS, James F. and S. A. BYRAM
     11 February 1867. Volume II, page 367.

DOSS, Mark and Emily COLBURN
     22 January 1842. Volume I, page 92.

DOVER, James M. and Hannah HOLCOMBE
     6 February 1866. Volume III, page 303.

DOYLE, John A. and Mary S. MOORE
     25 March 1859. Volume II, page 310.

DUCK, James S. and Nancy WEBSTER
     7 October 1841. Volume I, page 76.

DUKE, John F. and Elizabeth BURCHFIELD
30 August 1838.   Volume I, page 151.

DUKES, Henry M. and Angeline FALKNER
31 December 1857.   Volume II, page 302.

DUNÇAN, Harry and Sarah BAILY
28 November 1868.   Volume IV, page 83.

DUNKIN, William and Racheal BRASHER
24 December 1844.   Volume I, page 192.

DUNKIN, William L. and Mary Ann HAYS
21 October 1843.   Volume I, page 136.

DURAN, James H. and Elizabeth NELSON
28 December 1865.   Volume III, page 300.

EDWARDS, Isaac P. and Madeline GRIFFIN
19 October 1841.   Volume I, page 77.

EDWARDS, Isom and Frances SCOTT
3 June 1855.   Volume II, 197.

EDWARDS, J. R. and Mary STRAIN
5 December 1846.   Volume I, page 263.

ELDER, William G. and Harriett L. McGRAVER
4 January 1847.   Volume I, page 279.

ELESON, Richard and Catherine EDWARDS
28 December 1843.   Volume I, page 159.

ELLIOTT, Amos and Mary BRAGG
5 September 1848.   Volume I, page 303.

ELLIOTT, L. F. and Jane BRAGG
12 July 1853.   Volume II, page 102.

ELKINS, William and Frances A. TAYLOR
5 June 1844.   Volume I, page 180.

ELLENOR, James W. and Sarah MILLER
9 February 1843. Volume I, page 132.

ELLERSON, John E. and Marzly COKER
2 July 1841. Volume I, page 120.

ELLERSON, William M. and Emily McMILLON
29 April 1840. Volume I, page 42.

ELLIOTT, Allen and Caroline NUNNALLY
6 February 1843. Volume I, page 128.

ELLIOTT, Amos H. and Ann E. THOMPSON
11 July 1860. Volume III, page 97.

ELLIOTT, Amos M. and Sophronia HOLMAN
12 September 1861. Volume III, page 13

ELLIOTT, Bennett and Mary J. JONES
9 September 1855. Volume II, page 202.

ELLIOTT, Burnett and Eliza C. BRINKER
13 November 1846. Volume I, page 273.

ELLIOTT, Charles B. and Angeline FULTON
13 December 1846. Volume I, page 274.

ELLIOTT, George M. and Mary DILBANE
26 June 1844. Volume I, page 176.

ELLIOTT, James D. and Sophronia DAVIS
30 November1858. Volume II, page 354.

ELLIOTT, Hugh W. and Virginia JOHNSON
27 January 1864. Volume III, page 192.

ELLIOTT, Jefferson and Elizabeth BRASHER
12 December 1855. Volume II, page 215.

ELLIOTT, John and Jane Ann LEWIS
27 August 1851. Volume II, page 28.

ELLIOTT, Thomas A. and Mary E. HOSEY
    30 November 1856. Volume II, page 264.

ELLIOTT, William and Nancy BAKER
    3 December 1840. Volume I, page 52.

ELLISON, Samuel and Mary B. THOMAS
    8 November 1866. Volume III, page 349.

ENGLISH, Robert and Georgia SPAIGHT
    17 January 1849. Volume I, page 318.

ENGLISH, Z. and A. G. GARDNER
    27 December 1849. Volume I, page 350.

ERWIN, Joseph L. and Elizabeth McGRADY
    1 July 1858. Volume II, page 209.

ESSMAN, Thomas and Martha FULTON
    31 October 1844. Volume I, page 184.

EVANS, A. J. and Rebecca CASHATT
    16 April 1856. Volume II, page 258.

EVANS, Thomas G. and Joannah ARMSTRONG
    28 March 1858. Volume II, page 310.

FACKER, William and Barthama BATES
    16 September 1847. Volume I, page 286.

FANCHER, Thornton and Harriett LEMLEY
    14 January 1844. Volume I, page 164.

FANCHER, Pleasant M. and Hannah B. WARE
    1 November 1842. Volume I, page 179.

FANCHER, Samuel and Loucinda LEMLEY
    10 February 1846. Volume I, page 233.

FARLEE, William and Martha ALLEN
    24 October 1843, Volume I, page 165.

FARLEY, Daniel and Racheal REDDING
15 August 1853. Volume II, page 105.

FARLEY, Matthew A. and Chistany NABORS
30 November 1841. Volume I, page 100.

FARLEY, Matthew A. and Adaline N. PITTS
21 November 1853. Volume II, page 128.

FARLEY, William and Milley HENDERSON
21 January 1841. Volume I, page 54.

FARMER, John and Virginia Ann PEYTON
15 February 1852. volume II, page 49.

FARR, James W. and Susannah CROSS
11 January 1847. Volume I, page 276.

FARR, M.William and Margaret M. BARRETTE
8 April 1852. Volume II, page 52.

FARRELL, James T. and Sarah E. PAYNE
28 December 1858. Volume II, page 353.

FARRINGTON, John and Nancy BUTLER
20 December 1860. Volume III, page 119

FARSHEE, Hugh H. and Mary Ann LITTLETON
29 January 1848. Volume I, page 294.

FAUCETT, Henry and Sarah TENNY
26 October 1852. Volume II, page 34.

FAUST, John and Sophia Ann NASH
8 May 1851. Volume II, page 27.

FAUST, Miles G. and Nancy L. LAWLEY
20 January 1861. Volume III, page 116.

FERRELL, A. P. and Mary COLLINS
19 June 1853. Volume II, page 204.

FERRELL, Andrew J. and Jane LEATHERWOOD
26 September 1855. Volume II, page 208.

FERRELL, Francis M. and Martha JONES
27 January 1853. Volume II, page 84.

FIELDS, John T. and Winefield GRIFFIN
23 July 1846. Volume I, page 252.

FINCHER, John P. and Charlotte CROSS
14 September 1843. Volume I, page 144.

FINDLEY, James and Martha FLIPPIN
19 December 1841. Volume I, page 95.

FINLEY, Francis and Laura T. SCOTT
26 May 1852. Volume II, page 59.

FLEMING, A. T. and Nancy J. LITTLE
12 April 1860. Volume III, page 88.

FLAREGO, Henry E. and Sarah C. BIRCHFIELD
28 June 1861. Volume III, page 176.

FLETCHER, George A. and Nancy STEELE
9 February 1846. Volume I, page 228.

FLETCHER, John F. and Tibitha RACKLY
19 September 1854. Volume II, page 155.

FLIPPEN, Robert L. and Mary F. TUBMAN
23 September 1858. Volume II, page 335.

FLOREY, John W. and Mary S. HATCHER
1 November 1855. Volume II, page 218.

FORSHEA, Oliver and Nancy SMITH
24 August 1845. Volume I, page 214.

FOSTER, Elijah and Jane WHATLEY
3 May 1855. Volume II, page 192.

FOSTER, John and R. BURRELL
    10 November 1853.   Volume II, page 128.

FOUST, James A. and Franes C. NASH
    12 November 1841.   Volume I, page 83.

FOUST, Miles and Martha NASH
    26 October 1841.   Volume I, page 80.

FOWLEY, John W. and Lucinda LITTLETON
    15 September 1857.   volume II, page 296

FOX, Martin and Pheobe WOMACK
    5 November 1856.   Volume II, page 266.

FOX, Rufus E. and Agnes G. FARLEY
    11 November 1841.

FOX, William and J. K. GREGG
    10 December 1840.   Volume I, page 59.

FREEMAN, Thomas J. and Missouri CRIM
    9 November 1854.   Volume II, page 168.

FREEMAN, Thomas J. and Elivia THOMAS
    8 October 1857.   Volume II, page 297.

FROST, Thomas and Parthena WHORTON
    31 August 1845.   Volume I, page 214.

FULTON, John and Elizabeth WATSON
    27 April 1851.   volume II, page 20.

FUNDERBURG, Peter and Harriett SEALE
    25 December 1849.   Volume I, page 347.

GALLAWAY, Granderson and Susan MULLENDORE
    10 January 1844.

GALLAWAY, William and Catherine LAWLEY
    13 October 1844.   Volume I, page 187.

GALLOWAY, Miles and Ellen MINK
3 March 1840. Volume I, page 41.

GALLOWAY, R. A. and Mary BOZEMAN
23 April 1868. Volume IV, page 194.

GAMBLE, James M. and Agmore ROBERTSON
1 November 1855. Volume II, page 223.

GARDNER, B. and Mary POWELL
11 March 1848. Volume I, page 311.

GARDNER, Daniel and Elizabeth MOORE
25 September 1842. Volume I, page 113.

GARDNER, Dolphin and Caroline HALL
27 September 1846. Volume I, page 277.

GARDNER, James and Sarah FARR
20 February 1851. Volume II, page 29.

GARDNER, Thomas J. and Ella SEALE
11 November 1860. Volune III, page 109.

GARNER, Bradley and Ellen BOOTH
6 May 1841. Volume I, page 67.

GARNER, John and W Elizabeth WALKER
2 August 1827. Volume I, page 18.

GATLIN, Garrett and Ann C. RYAN
7 November 1842. Volume I, page 122.

GENTRY, Allen and Sebrina Jane GALLAWAY
16 January 1844. Volume I, page 163.

GENTRY, Larkin and Francis GAUSE
1 August 1852. Volume II, page 61.

GENTRY, Lewis and Mary Ann SWINNEY
3 May 1848. Volume I, page 296.

GEORGE, Dennis D. and Sarah Ann OGLESBERRY
9 October 1850. Volume II, page 23.

GEORGE, James and Sarah C. JONES
3 September 1854. Volume II, page 161.

GEORGE, James and Amanda L. PELL
8 January 1846. Volume I, page 237.

GEORGE L. and Mary Ann NICHOLS
25 December 1849. Volume I, page 348.

GEORGE, Rueben and Nancy ABERNATHY
4 October 1844. Volume I, page 183.

GETTENT, Simpson and Julia Ann KENDRICK
28 November 1848. Volume I, page 342.

GIBSON, Austin and Sarah CRIM
16 January 1840. Volume I, page 31.

GILBERT, James L. and Nancy BYARS
25 December 1856. Volume II, page 266.

GILBERT, William C. and Eleanor JOHNSON
18 August 1847. Volume I, page 284.

GILES, Martin and Rebecca ROBERTSON
23 February 1854. Volume II, page 143.

GILL, William and Annie GOODLIN
5 November 1865. Volume III, page 282.

GININ, W. L. and Nancy LITTLETON
16 December 1865. Volume III, page 290

GLASCOCK, Benjamin and Tempy HONEYCUTT
18 September 1856. Volume II, page 258

GLASCOCK, George and Martha A. BULLOCK
5 December 1861. Volume III, page 146.

GLASCOCK, William and Lucy ROBINTON
7 November 1850. Volume II, page 8.

GLASCOCK, Calvin and Martha ROBINTON
7 November 1850. Volume II, page 7.

GLASSOCK, Samuel and Elby COLUM
26 December 1849. Volume I, page 345.

GLOVER, Benjamin and Mary W. BAILEY
6 March 1850. Volume I, page 349.

GLOVER, Benjamin and A. COOPER
8 April 1866. Volume III, page 318.

GOGGINS, William and Eliza GARNER
22 November 1848. Volume I, page 308.

GOING, Pleasant and L. WEBB
25 August 1846. Volume I, page 253.

GOODENAUGH, Horatio and Josephine KIDD
11 December 1851. Volume II, page 40.

GOODGAME, F. C. and Margaret VANN
11 March 1852. Volume II, page 103.

GOODGAME, Robert and Sarah J. VINES
21 June 1860. Volume III, page 95.

GOODSON, Jasper and Susan G. LEE
29 August 1854. Volume II, page 158.

GORE, Joseph and Manuroy GENTRY
23 January 1840. Volume I, page 33.

GOSS, James and L. DAVIS
7 January 1857. Volume II, page 304.

GOTHARD, George and Melissa GLASCOCK
19 March 1854. Volume II, page 145.

GOTHARD, John M. and Mary A. MARTIN
   10 August 1851. Volume II, page 42.

GOTHARD, William P. and C. A. GREEN
   12 July 1857. Volume II, page 292.

GOTTON, Washington and Clementine JEMISON
   6 January 1859. Volume II, page 365.

GRAGG, Jonathan and Mary MULLINS
   14 January 1840. Volume I, page 32.

GRASTY, George S. and Mary Ann BRINKER
   6 June 1845. Volume I, page 194.

GRAY, John and Jane McGAGHRON
   10 March 1844. Volume I, page 167.

GREEN, Andrew and Nancy M. DUNLAP
   22 February 1846. Volume I, page 238.

GREEN, Charles and Everline SLOANE
   18 December 1839. Volume I, page 24.

GREEN Elias F. and Eleanor BUSBY
   2 April 1854. Volume II, page 146.

GREEN, Hanson and Cyntha MERRELL
   8 August 1844. Volume I, page 197.

GREEN, Samuel and Martha CARDWELL
   5 October 1856. Volume II, page 265.

GREEN, Silas and Laura HUGHES
   10 October 1861. Volume III, page 141.

GREEN, William and Nancy DENNIS
   8 January 1857. Volume II, page 267.

GREEN, Wyatt and Charity Ann GOTHARD
   13 April 1845. Volume I, page 200.

GREGORY, John and Nancy LITTLETON
18 January 1853. Volume II, page 43.

GRIFFIN, Clement and Elizabeth GOGGINS
31 December 1855. Volume II, page 173.

GRIFFIN, John A. and Malinda BURGESS
8 July 1847. Volume I, page 251.

GRIFFIN, Richard S. and Mary M. CROSS
22 December 1842. Volume I, page 118.

GROSE, Clodius and Martha Ann BAKER
23 December 1845. Volume I, page 230.

GUIN, Jonathan and Sonna COMER
2 November 1848. Volume I, page 307.

GUY, Joseph and Louisa GLASCOCK
8 June 1842. Volume I, page 105.

GUY, Joseph and Sarah PITTMAN
1 October 1840. Volume I, page 46.

GUY, William and Lucinda F. WILLIAMS
3 September 1857. Volume II, page 295.

HAGGARD, Henry and Margaret MITCHELL
4 March 1850. Volume I, page 339.

HAIL, Lindsey and Nancy MARTIN
15 November 1839. Volume I, page 57.

HAIL, Thomas and Martha LOGAN
8 September 1858. Volume II, page 335.

HAIL, William and Eliza HAIL
5 May 1852. Volume II, page 54.

HALE, T. J. and Martha POWELL
29 December 1846. Volume I, page 269.

HALL, Carter T. and Embrey BLOXSTON
26 April 1845.   Volume I, page 241.

HALL, James and Mary PRICE
9 January 1849.   Volume I, page 319.

HALL, John and Frances VICE
4 April 1849.   Volume I, page 331.   Apr:

HALL, William and Sophia KELLEY
23 October 1841.   Volume I, page 79.

HAMILTON, J. T. and Belinda GENTRY
5 April 1840.   Volume I, page 38.

HAMILTON, Thomas and Caroline NETTLES
10 September 1849.   Volume I, page 332.

HAMMELTON, Washington and Lucy HAMMELTON
24 November 1833.   Volume I, page 109.

HAMMOND, John G. and Lenora E. GOOCH
17 August 1852.   Volume II, page 63

HAND, Howard and Elizabeth PORTER
21 December 1847.   Volume I, page 290.

HAND, William A. and M. G. PATE
11 October 1846.   Volume I, page 278.

HANNAH, Samuel and Mary H. THOMPSON
28 September 1856.   Volume II, page 264

HANNAH, William M. and Martha Ann BEVELL
17 September 1856.   Volume II, page 273

HARDIMAN, Thomas and Nancy COBB
8 April 1852.   Volume II, page 56.

HARDIN, J. and Sintha POSY
8 June 1854.   Volume II, page 151.

HARDING, George and Malinda DAVIS
27 October 1841. Volume I, page 78.

HARLEE, Charles C. and Sarah Moore
14 January 1858. Volume II, page 305.

HARLESS, Henry and Malinda FOUST
10 October 1841. Volume I, page 85.

HARLESS, Henry and Frances ALLEN
27 January 1862. Volume III, page 159.

HARLIS, George C. and Piety BUTLER
23 November 1843. Volume I, page 149.

HARMON, John and Sarah ESTES
10 August 1856. Volume II, page 257.

HARMON, Stephen and Mary STARNES
17 December 1841. Volume I, page 60.

HARPER, James and Harriett PATE
20 February 1845. Volume I, page 197.

HARPER, Joseph and Jane VICK
1 January 1856. Volume II, page 230.

HARPER, William C. and Elizabeth BRINKER
19 November 1845. Volume I, page 220.

HARRIS, Allen and Sarah WIDEMAN
28 January 1847. Volume I, page 266.

HARRIS, Buckner and Anna HUMPHRIES
20 May 1859. C Volume II, page 367.

HARRIS, Jonothan and Mittly Ann BEECHER
13 December 1855. Volume II, page 225.

HARRIS, Joshua and Mary CRIM
5 November 1853. Volume II, page 83.

HARRISON, Denis and Emily FORD
11 January 1842. C Volume I, page 124.

HARRISON, James R. and Charlotte HARLISS
23 August 1840. Volume I, page 85.

HARRISON, Joel and Martha WEEKS
22 March 1849. Volume I, page 355.

HARRISON, John W. and Permelia C. HARPER
6 January 1842. Volume I, page 97.

HARRISON, Thomas and Louisa L. HOUSTON
30 November 1845. Volume I, page 222.

HARRISON, William and Sarah TEAMAN
6 August 1846. Volume I, page 225.

HARVELL, George H. and Louisa BAYETT
12 f February 1847. Volume I, page 292.

HARVY, Patric and Sarah SEALE
9 February 1858. Volume II, page 311.

HATCHER, Demsey and Mary CASHATT
9 February 1845. Volume I, page 198.

HATLEY, William and Mary Ann MASON
10 August 1843, Volume I, page 139.

HAVIS, John and Pheobe Jane HARDING
23 December 1841. Volume I, page 91.

HAWKINS, Joshua and Layah COX
4 October 1852. Voluem II, page 75.

HEAD, William and Frances WARD
14 February 1843. Volume I, page 142.

HEATLEY, Coleman and Sarah WILLIAMS
25 March 1847. Volume I, page 259.

HEATLEY, James and Nancy ROBERTSON
    28 April 1842. Volume I, page 104.

HEDY, Julian and Elem BOOTH
    11 January 1847. Volume I, page 247.

HENDERSON, H. and Sarah HARMON
    10 August 1848. Volume I, page 300.

HENDERSON, Pleasant and Elizabeth SEAMAN
    12 March 1841. Volume I, page 66.

HENLEY, Jesse and Susan MARCUS
    12 January 1843. Volume I, page 131.

HILL, Allen and Margaret, FIELDS
    29 November 1849. Volume I, page 347.

HILL, Robert and Nancy MILLER
    9 November 1840. Volume I, page 51.

HILL, Thomas H. and Catherine LANGLEY
    3 January 1849. Volume I, page 319.

HILL, William and Susan ALPIN
    10 August 1841. Volume I, page 72.

HINDS, Frances A. and Dinsomore NEALY
    17 March 1844, Volume I, page 172.

HOLCOMB, Jesse and Susan Mary SAXON
    6 December 1846. Volume I, page 275.

HOLCOMB, William and Mary ST. CLAIR
    15 November 1852. Volume II, page 72.

HOLLIS, Reuben and Rhoda WATSON
    7 August 1846. Volume I, page 247.

HOLMES, William and Louisa RINEHART
    5 October 1843. Volume I, page 141.

HOLSOMBECK Derrick and Ellen LOLLEY
19 December 1844. Volume I, page 195.

HOLSOMBECK, John and Margaret LOLLEY
28 January 1844. Volume I, page 154.

HOLSOMBECK, Richard and Olive HOLSOMBECK
5 July 1857. Volume II, page 292.

HORTON, Ervin and Mary WILDER
16 February 1848. Volume I, page 298.

HORTON, Jonathan and Jemima REYNOLDS
5 October 1843. Volume I, page 141.

HORTON, M. J. and Mary E. ARNETT
11 August 1846. Volume I, page 125.

HORTON, Mirach and Navassa ARNETT
3 November 1840. Volume I, page 50.

HORTON, Thomas and Melvina POWELL
15 February 1849. Volume I, page 319.

HOWARD, William and Cinda GHOST
2 October 1839. Volume I, page 25.

HUCKABEE, Jonathan and Martha MILLS
3 February 1840. Volume I, page 57.

HUDSON, Jacob and Elizabeth BELL
3 February 1848. Volume I, page 297.

HUGHES, Alexander and Edney STINSON
27 February 1840. Volume I, page 34.

HUGHES, James and Julia E. VICK
28 January 1841. Volume I, page 56.

HUNICUTT, Zachariah and Charity WHATLEY
2 February 1844. Volume I, page 155.

HUTSON, Abraham and Jane A. HOWARD
19 June 1850. Volume I, page 324.

ISBELL, Hugh and Elizabeth HOLMES
26 October 1848. Volume I, page 305.

ISBELL, Robert and Elizabeth LOVE
28 July 1840. Volume I, page 97.

JOHNS, John and Sarah PICKENS
26 January 1840. Volume I, page 41.

JOHNSON, A. and C. C. SMITH
23 January 1847. Volume I, page 251.

JOHNSON, Benjamin and Sarah McCLANDON
15 January 1823. Volume I, page 33.

JOHNSON, Isaac and Catherine Galloway
11 October 1849. Volume I, page 326.

JOHNSON, Isaac and Martha RUSSELL
9 October 1851. Volume II, page 35.

JOHNSON, J. D. and Sarah Ann McKEE
4 September 1849. Volume I, page 349.

JOHNSON, J. M. and Rebbeca GHOST
26 January 1847. Volume I, page 274.

JOHNSON, Jacob and Rebecca MORRIS
29 September 1824. Volume I, page 2.

JOHNSON, James and Fanny LINDSEY
21 June 1849. Volume I, page 343.

JOHNSON, James and A. B. NELSON
9 December 1841. Volume I, page 88.

JOHNSON, Jesse and Mary A. DeSHAZO
27 January 1847. Volume I, page 271.

JOHNSON, John and Polly PRICE
    21 August 1827. Volume I, page 19.

JOHNSON, Moses and Mary KELLY
    11 January 1847. Volume I, page 336.

JOHNSON, Moses and Nancy LITTLEPAGE
    26 May 1842. Volume 106.

JOHNSON, Obediah and Nancy JOHNSTON
    8 July 1840. Volume I, page 58.

JOHNSTON, Samuel and Elizabeth DUNKIN
    23 March 1845. Volume 8, page 210.

JOLLEY, William and Sarah GRADY
    21 November 1847. Volume I, page 288.

JOLLEY, William and Mary CRAWFORD
    29 December 1842. Volume I, page 119.

JONES, A. and S. CRUMPTON
    18 February 1849. Volume I, page 316.

JONES, DAVID AND Nancy DURAN
    10 March 1841. volume I, page 62.

JONES, G. H. and Sarah Jane MOORE
    16 September 1849. Volume II, page 2.

JONES, Henry and Mary Elizabeth BAILEY
    18 December 1849. Volume I, page 334.

JONES, James and Sarah H. CHILDERS
    4 April 1843. Volume I, page 133.

JONES, John and Mary C. STREET
    2 May 1844. Volume I, page 174.

JONES, Lewis and Minerva McCLENDON
    26 September 1850. Volume I, page 359.

JONES, Martin and Kezia BUSBY
  10 December 1840. Volume I, page 59.

JONES, Nathan and Winney BAILEY
  31 March 1840. volume I, page 38.

JONES, Sanders and JUdea Ann STREET
  2 December 1841. Volume I, page 86.

JONES, William and Elizabeth FOSHEE
  7 December 1841. Volume I, page 88,

KENDRICK, Isom and Elmira C. GILBERT
  19 October 1845. C Volume I, page 234.

KIDD, John and Eveline MOORE
  24 April 1842. Volume I, page 104.

KIDD, Webb and Mary A. NELSON
  10 December 1840. Volume I, page 89.

KIDD, William T. and R. M. MITCHELL
  10 July 1849. Volume II, page 2.

KING, Benjamin and Dorothy MULLENEZ
  31 May 1840. Volume I, page 42.

KYKINDALL, Joseph and Rody JOHNSTON
  27 September 1849. Volume I, page 336.

LACY, James and Sarah MERIDETH
  16 November 1851. Volume I, page 92.

LAWLEY, Elijah and Sarah BAKER
  3 November 1839. Volume I, page 87.

LAWLEY, Elisha and Caroline DAVIS
  22 July 1847. Volume I, page 284.

LAWLEY, John and Permelia ARMSTRONG
  17 October 1847. Volume I, page 288.

LAWLEY, Lewis and Louisa CASHATT
    24 September 1845.   Volume I, page 245.

LAWRENCE, THOMAS P. and Rachel ELLIOTT
    25 March 1842.   Volume I, page 103.

LEDBETTER, Moses and Eleanor MUSE
    19 September 1844.   Volume I, page 161.

LEE, Greogory and Lucinda LEE
    30 September 1841.   Volume I, page 81.

LEE, Irgram and Julia STREET
    20 February 1827.   Volume I, page 13.

LEE, James and Barchaby BAILEY
    14 September 1841.   Volume I, page 180.

LEE, Jiles and Ann WALKER
    28 February 1844.   Volume I, page 175.

LEMORE, Willis and Nargaret GAMBOL   Mar
    18 December 1845.   Volume I, page 225.

LESLEY, Joseph and Louisa PAGE
    29 January 1846.   Volume I,p 236.

LESTER, Charles and Ann E. MOORE
    22 July 1846.   Volume I, page 267.

LESTER, John H. and Henrietta HARPER
    15 September 1846.   Volume I, page 253.

LEWIS, J. E. and Elizabeth LEWIS
    17 December 1844.   Volume I, page 227.

LEWIS, JOhn T. and Mary E. BEVILL
    13 June 1849.   Volume I, page 330.

LEWIS, John W. and Caroline J. CAMPBELL
    13 June 1839.   Volume I, page 142.

LINDSEY, Charles and Lucy MERRILL
21 March 1846. Volume I, page 232.

LINDSEY, David and N. W. CROSS
9 April 1840. Volume I, page 39.

LINDSEY, Eliha and Mary T. NASH
1 May 1845. Volume I, page 203.

LINDSEY, William and Nancy MERRILL
10 June 1845. Volume I, page 204.

LINSEY, John and Polly SKILLMAN
2 February 1827. Volume I, page 10.

LITTLETON, Wilson and Keziah M. GUY
7 July 1841. volume I, page 74.

LOLLEY, Avery and Eliza PITTS
28 December 1839. Volume I, page 29.

LOLLEY, Henry and Elizabeth GASHATT
22 July 1849. Volume I, page 342.

LOLLEY, Henry and Susan MORRIS
23 September 1841. volume I, page 76.

LOLLEY, Levi and Elizabeth HUTCHIN
30 May 1849. Volume I, page 341.

LOUCUS, William and Froney LOLLEY
31 december 1840. Volume I, page 53.

LOVE, Allen and Mary BEAN
26 March 1843. Volume I, page 132.

LOVELADY, Elijah and Nancy LUCAS
27 July 1843. Volume I, page 140.

LOWERY, Thomas and Martha CAMERON
22 September 1825. Volume I, page 4.

LUCAS, James and Tabitha WEEKS
10 January 1844. Volume I, page 158.

LUCAS, Abraham, and Nancy LAWLEY
4 October 1848. Volume I, page 306.

LUCAS, John and Mary A. LOLLEY
4 March 1841. Volume I, page 61.

LUCAS, Solomon and Frances WEEKS
23 January 1845. Volume I, page 199.

LUCUS, Thomas and Elizabeth WALKER
11 July 1849. Volume I, page 349.

LUCUS, William and Nancy GOSHATT
4 December 1846. Volume I, page 276.

LUSLEY, Francis and Matilda POGUE
9 February 1843. Volume I, page 126.

LYON, John and Ann M. TEAGUE
6 September 1827. Volume I, page 20.

McADAMS, Isaac and Elizabeth SENTELL
25 December 1845. volume I, page 232.

McBRIDE, David and Louisa N. FOUST
9 March 1845. Volune I, page 22o.

McBRYDE, Henry and Charlotte BUTLER
18 September 1845. Volume I, page 223.

McCLANAHAN, D. N. and Caroline REEVES
12 January 1847. Volume I, page 261,

McCLANAHAN, David N. and Charlotte ROPPER
12 April 1841. Volume I, page 64.

McCLANAHAN, Samuel and Emiley RUSHING
16 January 1842. Volume I, page 94.

McCLINTON, Drew W. and Mary A. FLIPPin
15 May 1840. Volume I, page 134.

McCLINTON, James B. and Catherine MORRISON
12 August 1841. Volume I, page 84.

McCOLISTER, A. C. and Louisa DAVIS
19 August 1845. Volume I, page 22 2.

McCORMICK, Hugh and Amanda BAKER
26 May 1846. Volume I, page 183.

McHAHEE, Samuel and Charlotte CLARK
9 November 1849. Volume I, page 354.

McGEE, J. A. and Nancy Ann WADDLE
28 September 1848. Volume I, page 303.

McGINNIS, R. and Mary E. WILLIAMSON
1 March 1849. Volume I, page 313.

McGRAW, Silas and Mary J. SCOTT
6 June 1844. Volume I, page 182.

McHENRY, J. W. and Jane PRICE
27 February 1849. Volume I, page 313.

McKINNEY, John P. and Mary GREEN
8 April 1841. Volume I, page 63.

McLEROY, Ramson and Frances E. HILL
2 March 1845. Volume I, page 226.

McWILLIAMS, William and Elizabeth NABORS
26 February 1844. Volume I, page 164.

MADDOX, William and Mary RIGGINS
11 September 1842. Volume I, page 111.

MARDIS, William and Matilda ROBERTSON
23 August 1827. Volume I, page 15.

MARCUS, Elisha and Susan BATES
20 July 1841. Volume I, page 72.

MARKIS, John and Ann ATKINSON
12 March 1849. Volume I, page 344.

MARONEY, Middleton, and Elizabeth LAWLER
29 January 1827. Volume I, page 17.

MARONY, Phillip and Martha RICHARDSON
27 September 1846. Volume I, page 248.

MARTIN, Bartly and Mary Ann GENTRY
15 February 1949. Volume I, page 323.

MARTIN, Isaac N. and Elizabeth LITTLEFIELI
5 September 1849. Volume I, page 338.

MARTIN, John C. and Eliza NETTLES
9 August 1840. Volume I, page 40.

MARTIN, Mathew and Racheal RUSSELL
27 December 1849. Volume I, page 337.

MARTIN, Robert and Elizabeth CRIM
12 October 1843. Volume I, page 150.

MARTIN, Warren and Huldey, GENTRY
3 May 1846. Volume I, page 228.

MARTIN, William C. and Martha Ann WILLIAMS
22 June 1845. Volume I, page 204.

MASON, George and Lucinda POST
6 February 1845. Volume I, page 196.

MASON, James and Elira EDWARDS
21 April 1840. Volume I, page 39.

MATHIS, John and Mary COMER
5 November 1845. Volume I, page 184.

MATTHEWS, John and Lethy MILES
7 December 1842. Volume I, page 130.

MEREDITH, P. W. and Eveline BENTON
10 December 1848. Volume I, page 309.

MERRELL, Richard and Darcas WILLIAMS
5 December 1847. Volume I, page 287.

MERRILL, William and Priscilla WILLIAMS
15 March 1849. Volume I, page 353.

MERRELL, Charles and Emily QUINN
20 February 1840. Volume I, page 36.

MERRELL, Wiley and Frances MASON
3 September 1846. Volume I, page 256.

MIDDLETON, Andrew J. and Mary Ann BAKER
29 June 1842. Volune I, page 105.

MILENDER, Jacob and Cinderall WATSON
13 July 1848. Volume I, page 299.

MILLER, Daniel and Martha S. DULRUMPLE
7 December 1845. Volume I, page 227.

MILLS, William and Elizabeth COBB
14 September 1848. Volume I, page 302.

MIMS, Elijah and Milley T. GOODGAME
7 December 1848. Volume I, page 309.

MINK, Jacob and Patty NETTLES
14 November 1841. Volume I, page 87.

MINK, James and Aviline GALLOWAY
26 March 1840. Volume I, page 40.

MITCHELL, Benjamin and Rachel GRAY
7 November 1826. Volume I, page 11.

MOATS, Simeon and Nancy JOHNSON
5 February 1846. Volume I, page 231.

MONK, John and Martha FORSHEE
19 February 1848. Volume I, page 304.

MOODY, Washington and Elizabeth BOWDEN
11 May 1841. Volume I, page 67.

MOORE, Alexander and Elizabeth ELLIOTT
22 February 1846. Volume I, page 240.

MOORE, Blanton and Martha SEALE
19 September 1839. Volume I, page 25.

MOORE, George and Amelia SEALE
16 November 1845. Volume I, page 218.

MOORE, Isaac and Nancy L. LOVELADY
11 January 1847. Volume I, page 268.

MOORE, James D. and HariettWOODRUFF
16 February 1841 Volume I, page 61.

MOORE, Pleasant and Rebecca FANCHER
24 February 1849. Volume I, page 315.

MOORE, William and Eleanor BAILEY
6 July 1843. Volume I, page 135.

MOORE, W. Alexander and Minerva MOORE
7 December 1843. Volume I, page 148.

MORGAN Hugh and Bethiah WATSON
16 April 1843. Volume I, page 133.

MORGAN, W. M. and Catherine NOBB
28 January 1847. Volume I, page 263.

MORRIS, Elijah and Seney RICHEY
7 January 1847. Volume I, page 273.

MOSELY, Peedles and Mahala GOOCH
21 October 1845.   Volume I, page 212.

MOSTILLO, Sanford and Rebecca NABORS
21 Jaunary 1840.   Volume I, page 30.

MOTES, John D. and Mary JOHNSON
3 November 1854.   Volume II, page 167.

MULLINS, Arthur and Martha COOPER
26 September 1841.   Volume I, page 75.

MUNAY, James N. and Eleanor GALLOWAY
21 August 1845.   Volume I, page 206.

MUNDINE, Charles and Anna HUNTSMAN
16 April 1826.   Volume I, page 0.

MUSE, John and Susan MASON
28 October 1845.   Volume I, page 221.

MUSE, Willis and Elizabeth J. MASON
2 March 1844.   Volume I, page 168.

NABORS, John H. and Susan C. McHENRY
2 December 1847.   Volume I, page 289.

NABORS, L. J. and matilda BAILEY
16 February 1843.   Volume I, page 127.

NASH, Thomas F. and Louisa MORRIS
1 February 1849.   Volume I, page 320.

NEALY, Dinsmore and Frances HINDS
17 March 1844.   Volume I, page 172.

NEALY, Joseph D. and Frances BOUDEN
13 July 1843.   Volume I, page 138.

NELSON, Alexander and Mary E. POWELL
3 April 1844.   Volume I, page 176.

NELSON, Andrew and J. S. JOHNSON
    9 December 1841. Volume I, page 88.

NELSON, Francis A. and Parrellee ELLIOTT
    19 January 1843. Volume I, page 125.

NELSON, Hardy and Sarah ELLIOTT
    17 September 1846. Volume I, page 243.

NELSON, Simpson and Nancy ELLIOTT
    6 July 1843. Volume I, page 138.

NICKLES, Wilson and Martha REDDING
    20 January 1842. Volume I, page 98.

NICKLES, John and Jane HARMON
    24 August 1848. Volume I, page 302

NIVENS, Jesse and Susan Jane TICER
    24 January 1843. Volume I, page 125.

NOLING, James and Mary ROLLINGS
    24 March 1845. Volume I, page 205.

NORRIS, Nathan and Mary Ann LESTER
    12 October 1844. Volume I, page 188.

NORRIS, William B. and Nancy SUDBERRY
    15 January 1846. Volume I, page 233.

NORTHCUTT, James and Nancy Ann MORRIS
    7 October 1849. Volume I, page 344.

NUNLEY, W. G. and Zelpha GRIFFIN
    17 February 1849. Volume II, page 7.

NUNNALLY, William and Sarah BLACKSBY
    19 January 1845. Volume I, page 207.

OGLESBURG, John and Elizabeth CHAMPION
    22 January 1850. Volume I, page 354.

O'HARA, James C. and Eleanor S. TEAGUE
24 August 1843. Volume I, page 140.

O'NEAL, John R. and Rebecca SAXON
27 October 1846. Volume I, page 277.

ORR, Robert and Martha CROWSON
28 November 1839. Volume I, page 26.

OSLEY, Thomas and Zilpha BAILEY
5 August 1844. Volume I, page 173.

OVERTON, David and Racie M. JOHNSON
2 February 1847. Volume I, page 266.

OVERTON, Jack S. and Martha PLEDGER
14 September 1846. Volume I, page 279.

OVERTON, Jesse and Sarah Jane BAILEY
7 October 1839. Volume I, page 79.

OZLEY, George and Lucy BROWN
15 June 1843. Volume I, page 136.

OZLEY, Gilbert and Theny COST.
20 January 1846. Volume I, page 257.

OZLEY, Seaborn and Louisa CRUMP
1 January 1845. Volume I, page 225.

OZLEY, Sebron and Adaline OLDHAM
7 January 1840. Volume I, page 37.

PACE, William and Jane KEMP
16 January 1849. Volume I, page 3.

PAINE, Hermes and Nancy BUTLER
5 October 1842. Volume I, page 114.

PARKER, Herman and Jane JORDAN
14 September 1845. Volume I, page 255.

PARNELL, Alba and Virginia REINHARDT
24 October 1849. Volume I, page 329.

PATE, George and Martha J. GLENN
12 February 1846. Volume I, page 236.

PATE, James and Lindy SCARBOROUGH
11 July 1849. Volume I, page 256.

PATTERSON, John H. and Mary M. TAYLOR
24 December 1846. Volume I, page 270.

PAYNE, Calvin and Malinda ROBERTSON
25 November 1841. Volume I, page 96.

PAYNE, Calvin and Samantha HUGHS
16 December 1849. Volume I, page 351.

PAYNE, L. and Ann PAYNE
20 February 1844. Volume I, page 162.

PEARSON, Jonathan and Clarissa AVERY
17 October 1848. Volume I, page 306.

PICKENS, Isreal and Nancy BIRDING
9 October 1848. Volume I, page 305.

PICKENS, John S. and Eliza SMITH
6 August 1844. Volume I, page 175.

PICKET, James and Elizabeth BOOTHE
26 March 1843, Volume I, page 129.

PILGREEN, Elias and Rechel CRIM
11 December 1834. Volume I, page 21.

PITTS, Robert and Adaline DESHAZOR
24 September 1846. Volume I, page 334.

PITTS, William and Permelia C. NICHOLAS
4March 1847. Volume I, page 265.

POINDEXTER, Benjamin and Mary A. HARPER
28 July 1840. Volume I, page 43.

POINDEXTER, Robert W. and Harriett NUNNALLY
21 January 1844. Volume I, page 153.

POPE, Willie H. and Caroline McHENRY
28 November 1844. Volume I, page 185.

PORTER E. and Rhoda PORTER
22 April 1847. Volume I, page 272.

PORTER, Jackson and Mary Ann SEALE
6 January 1848. Volume I, page 293.

PORTER, John A. and Roame WOODRUFF
6 July 1843. Volume I, page 136.

PORTER, Washington and Syntha MUSICK
11 January 1844. Volume I, page 151.

POSEY, Alexander and Harriett MARTIN
26 January 1844. Volume I, page 160.

POSEY, Stephen and Armanda MIDDLEBROOKS
31 October 1841. Volume I, page 93.

POSEY, Steven and Sarah FRASHER
6 February 1844. Volume I, page 160.

POST, David and Jane HARTLEY
2 March 1843. Volume I, page 127.

POST, William and Elizabeth McADAMS
8 December 1841. Volume I, page 89.

POSTON, Hugh R. and Rebecca PRINTICE
25 March 1839. Volume I, page 27.

PRENTICE, William and Elizabeth MARTIN
12 December 1842. Volume I, page 118.

PRICE, George and Sarah F. MOORE
   15 October 1845. Volume I, page 205.

PRICE, John and Bical BARRETT
   21 July 1844. Volume I, page 174.

PRUITT, Jacob and Lucy R. MOSS
   10 November 1842. Volume I, page 120.

PUCKETT, Hasting and Caroline HORTON
   29 October 1840. Volume I, page 49.

PUCKETT, Waitus and Eliza McELROY
   11 May 1841. Volume I, page 68.

QUINN, William and Margaret MOORE
   21 March 1850. Volume II, page 9.

RAGSDALE, John R. and Nancy PERRY
   30 October 1845. Volume I, page 242.

RALEIGH, William and Epha McLEOD
   3 May 1849. Volume II, page 1.

RAMSEY, Alleroson and Eliza JOHNSON
   11 October 1839. Volume I, page 26.

RAMEY, Ramson and Katherine LESTER
   2 July 1843. Volume I, page 136.

RANDALL, Benjamin F. and Nancy WILSON
   22 January 1822. Volume I, page 29.

RANDALL, George and Elizabeth RICHARDSON
   27 October 1841. Volume I, page 49.

RASBERRY, James and Irma HAYES
   16 April 1842. Volume I, page 103.

RASBERRY, Thomas and Mary HAYES
   7 August 1848. Volume I, page 301.

RAY, James and Christian BRASHER
25 January 1827. Volume I, page 12.

RAY, James and Lucinda COLLUM
6 January 1848. Volume I, page 295.

REA, Thomas and Eliza SHELTON
18 October 1842. Volume I, page 123.

RHODES, William C. and Sarah F. LEWIS
26 March 1840. Volume I, page 37.

RHODES, William C. and Elizabeth A.
WILLIAMSON. 12 July 1844. Vol. I,p.171.

RICHARDSON, James L. and Catherine GRAY
23 August 1842, Volume I, page 111.

RICHARDSON, Robert C. and Eliza BLASINGUM
18 April 1846. Volume I, page 244.

RINDHART, Nicholas and Mary G. BUSBY
26 February 1843. Volume I, page 128.

REACH, John and Martha J. BUTLER
6 December 1849. Volume I, page 335.

ROBERSON, Elisha and Samantha MILLS
20 May 1845. Volume I, page 209.

ROBINSON, John and Armada STAMPS
29 June 1848. Volume I, page 297.

ROBINSON, Richard and Jane E. THOMAS
11 July 1847. Volume I, page 246.

ROBERSON, Arthur and Elizabeth LINDSEY
16 August 1840. Volume I, page 45.

ROBERTSON, Bobb and Sarah RAY
11 July 1846. Volume I, page 147.

ROBERTSON, David and Avaline SNELL
2 October 1843. Volume I, page 146.

ROBERTSON, Elisha and Marilza MILLER
13 September 1827. Volume I, page 21.

ROBERTON, George W. and Martha LITTLETON
2 December 1840. Volume I, page 49.

ROBERTSON, Henry and Priscilla McGOWAN
28 January 1841. Volume I, page 55.

ROBERTSON, James and Mahuldy SKELTON
1834. Volume I, page 82.

ROBERTSON, James H. and OZLEY, Caroline
15 November 1842. Volume I, page 119.

ROBERTSON, John and Margaret MARTIN
14 April 1843, Volume I, page 137.

ROBERTSON, William and Margaret HEADLY
11 April 1847. Volume I, page 267.

ROGERS, William and Renvey MOORE
4 April 1844. Volume I, page 169.

RUNNELS, James L. and Elizabeth MOORE
5 December: 1839. Volume I, page 28.

RUSHING, Robert R. and Sophia SAWYERS
18 November 1841. volume I, page 83.

RUSHING, William and Mary D. SAWYER
22 September 1840. Volume I, page 45.

RUSSELL, John and Nancy WALLS
29 July 1848. Volume I, page 299.

RUSSELL, Wiley and Louisa OLDHAM
25 October 1844. Volume I, page 192.

RUSSELL, William and Sarah HOLCOMB
    15 January 1845. Volume I, page 189.

SAINE, Elisha and Sarah LAWRENCE
    10 February 1842. Volume I, page 99.

ST.John, William and Manerva Jane B, CROSS
    12 November 1843. Volume I, page 168.

SALSER, Samuel and E. MOORE
    18 December 1849. Volume I, page 346.

SAWYER, Elbert and Elizabeth Ann RUSHING
    18 January 1844. Volume I, page 152.

SCREVENOR, John P. and Elizabeth WALKER
    14 November 1842. Volume I, page 122.

SCREVENOR, Rubin and Mary JOHNSON
    26 September 1843. Volume I, page 144.

SEALE, Joshua and Susannah MOORE
    8 April 1847. volume I, page 189.

SEALE, Willaby and Sarah S. FORD
    18 March 1847. Volume I, page 258.

SEALE, Felix and Beedy C. CRIM
    16 January 1848. volume I, page 292.

SEALE, Herod and Christy HAWKINS
    12 December 1841. volume I, page 90.

SEALE, Robert and Mary J. WiLLIAMS
    24 December 1846. Volume I, page 260.

SHEELY, John and Lidia PEARCE
    8 November 1825. Volume I, page 8.

SHEPHERD, Robert and Elizabeth JOHNSON
    1 September 1825. Volume I, page 5.

SHIELDS, James and Sarah Ann CAVNESS
    29 September 1844. Volume I, page 181.

SHOLARS, Ramson and Sarah E. WALLACE
    16 May 1841. Volume I, page 69.

SHRADER, Henry and Frances NEAL
    29 August 1842. Volume I, page 110.

SIKES, Fredrick and Mary McCATHRIN
    22 September 1844. Volume I, page 180.

SIMES, Samuel and Rhoda JONES
    23 October 1842. Volume I, page 115.

SIMPSON, Thomas F. and Ducy WESTBROOK
    21 January 1827. Volume I, page 15.

SIMPSON, Thomas S. and Rebecca HAFFA
    19 September 1841. Volume I, page 107.

SINGLETON, John and Sarah HENDERSON
    23 December 1846. Volume I, page 284.

SIRRATT, John and Sarah DAVIS
    5 April 1846. Volume I, page 242.

SMITH, Benjamin and Maryann SMITH
    26 October 1845. Volume I, page 235.

SMITH, George and Syntha RICHEA
    11 August 1845. Volume I, page 216.

SMITH, Jesse and Priscilla LEATHERWOOD
    24 February 1842. Volume I, page 112.

SMITH, Thomas and Alsey BROWN
    23 May 1841. Volume I, page 68.

STEPHENS, Elijah and Lucretia JOHNSON
    6 August 1843. Volume I, page 139.

STEPHENS, Joseph and Elizabeth LEATHERWOOD
17 October 1839. Volume I, page 28.

STORES, John S. and Martha A. HAZZARD
31 December 1849. Volume I, page 330.

STOVALL, William P. and Linney McADAMS
5 September 1825. Volume I, page 1.

STRAISNER, Hiram and Lelia DUCK
18 February 1841. Volume I, page 55.

STREET, James and Matilda MAY
20 February 1827. Volume I, page 13.

SUMNER, Allen and Niceyany RICHEY
25 November 1844. Volume I, page 184.

TAYLOR, William J. and Jane DUNN
28 December 1847. Volume I, page 289.

TEAGUE, James and Mary E. BAKER
5 December 1842. Volume I, page 117.

TIDWELL, Joseph B. and Tebitha FOX
16 January 1845. Volume I, page 194.

TIDWELL, Peter B. and Jane TIDWELL
11 June 1825. Volume I, page 4.

TOPKINS, Thomas J. and Rebeca J. LAWLEY
11 October 1849. Volume I, page 325.

TOWNLEY, John and Sarah ACTON
19 May 1842. Volume I, page 112.

USSERY, George H. and Cinthaberry ACTON
5 June 1825. Volume I, page 3.

VANDIMAN, J. B. and Elizabeth ROBERTSON
17 November 1833. Volume I, page 109.

VEAZEY, Elzey and Juliann E. PRINTICE
20 February 1843. Volume I, page 152.

VEST, John L. and Martha ROBERTS
14 August 1841. volume I, page 73.

VICK, Alexander and Mary HAWKS
27 November 1843. Volume I, page 149.

VICK, Manuel and Henrietta HUGHES
9 January 1842. Volume I, page 96.

VICK, William and Abrigal HUGHES
25 November 1840. Volume I, page 48.

WAGGENOR, William and Priscilla ELLISON
20 February 1845. volume I, page 229.

WAGGONER, Henry and Elizabeth McKEE
10 January 1843. Volume I, page 131.

WALDROP, George W. and Elizabeth WILLIAMS
23 June 1841. volume I, page 69.

WALKER, John H. and Lucinda WATLEY
25 November 1848. Volume I, page 308.

WALKER, John L. and Malinda BRASHER
20 October 1848. Volume I, page 304.

WALKER, Robert L. and Narcissa BRAGG
15 February 1849. Volume I, page 315.

WALKER, Samuel and Elizabeth JOHNSON
5 November 1843. Volume I, page 145.

WALTON, J. G. and Nancy TURNER
24 December 1844. Volume I, page215,

WATERMAN, B. J. and Leah DUCK
21 February 1840. volume I, page 34.

WATLEY, Sid and V. J. GRAGG
7 March 1847. Volume I, page 244.

WATSON, Andrew J. and Lucy Ann GHOST
29 December 1841. Volume I, page 94.

WATSON, Jesse and Racheal HOLLESS
11 October 1844. Volume I, page 211.

WATSON, Samuel and Martha Ann BOWDON
1 October 1844. Volume I, page 178.

WEBSTER, John M. and Margaret MARTIN
5 July 1849. Volume I, page 339.

WELCH, William A. and Willie Ann WALLACE
12 October 1843. Volume I, page 143.

WELLS, Abner and Sarah CUNNINGHAM
13 March 1842. Volume I, page 102.

WEST, John P. and Mariah L. MILLS
28 August 1844. Volume I, page 210.

WEVER, Abraham and Judith ROWEN
4 February 1827. Volume I, page 10.

WHITE, James W. and Caroline RICHEY
10 December 1840. volume I, page 53.

WHITE, Pleasant and Jane ROBERTSON
18 October 1842. Volume I, page 116.

WHITFIELD, George W. and Mary KINDRICK
14 November 1841. Volume I, page 81.

WIDEMAN, John and Polly TIDWELL
7 August 1825. Volume I, page 6.

WILDER, Daniel and Susan J. NEVINS
25 January 1848. Volume I, page 294.

WILDER, James and Jane FORD
13 March 1845. Volume I, page 224.

WILLIAMS, Amos and Margie AUBRY
7 October 1849. Volume II, page 1.

WILLIAMS, Hartwell and Eliza SMITH
13 November 1849. Volume I, page 331.

WILLIAMS, Hilrey and Milley GREEN
15 June 1848. Volume I, page 295.

WILLIAMS, John A. and Sarah B. SENTELL
16 January 1841. Volume I, page 54.

WILLIAMS, Levy and Christian McCOLLISTER
21 September 1841. Volume I, page 75.

WILLIAMS, Robert and Milley E. WARD
29 October 1845. Volume I, page 215.

WILLIAMS, William and Mary N. RAGSDALE
25 January 1843. Volume I, page 126.

WILLIAMSON, James and Sarah SMOOT
4 July 1846. Volume I, page 71.

WILLIAMSON, James and Mary E. LEWIS
5 May 1845. Volume I, page 208.

WILLIAMSON, John and Clarissa BURCHFIELD
3 June 1845. volume I, page 231.

WILLIAMSON, R. B. and Eliza WRIGHT
1 December 1839. Volume I, page 30.

WILSON, Andrew and Jane McGUIRE
4 October 1825. Volume I, page 7.

WILSON, Littleton and Kiziah GUY
7 July 1841. Volume I, page 74.

WILSON, John W. and Elizbaeth E. LESTER
31 October 1842. Volume I, page 116.

WILSON, Thomas and Sarah HARKINS
15 October 1846. Volume I, page 278.

WILSON, Weston and Delilia C. DESMIRE
1 January 1843. Volume I, page 123.

WILSON, William A. and Zendrella MOORE
9 November 1841. Volume I, page 100.

WOOD, Edward and Mary JOURDON
8 June 1845. Volume I, page 200.

WOOD, Joseph and Martha LINDSEY
18 February 1847. Volume I, page 200.

WOOD, Willis and Qualla HAGART
4 May 1849. Volume II, page 18.

WYATT, William and Disa HAMON
20 April 1849. Volume I, page 350.

WYATT, Robert and Nancy PRENTICE
6 March 1842. Volume I, page 102.

YOUNG, William M. and Hariett ARNETT
23 January 1840. Volume I, page 32.

INDEX

A

B

G

H

X Y Z

None

www.ingramcontent.com/pod-product-compliance
Lightning Source LLC
Chambersburg PA
CBHW031132020426
42333CB00012B/336